P9-ECL-011

6/98

FIRST
BIOGRAPHIES

Nelson Mandela

Published by Raintree Steck-Vaughn Publishers, an imprint of Steck-Vaughn Company

Planned and produced by The Creative Publishing Company
Editors: Christine Lawrie and Pam Wells

Library of Congress Cataloging-in-Publication Data

Holland, Gini.
    Nelson Mandela / Gini Holland; illustrated by Mike White.
        p.   cm. — (First biographies)
    Summary: A biography of the son of a Thembu chief who became a civil rights activist, political prisoner, and president of South Africa.
    ISBN 0-8172-4454-9
    1. Mandela, Nelson, 1918- — Juvenile literature.   2. Presidents — South Africa — Biography — Juvenile literature.   3. South Africa — Politics and government — 1948- — Juvenile literature.   [1. Mandela, Nelson, 1918- .   2. Presidents — South Africa.   3. Civil rights workers. 4. Blacks — South Africa — Biography.]   I. White, Mike (Mike H.). 1939- ill.   II. Title.   III. Series.
    DT1949.M35H35   1997
    968.06'4'092 — dc20
    [B]

96-4299
CIP
AC

Printed and bound in the United States
1 2 3 4 5 6 7 8 9 0 W 99 98 97 96

FIRST
BIOGRAPHIES

Nelson Mandela

Gini Holland
Illustrated by Mike White

RSVP

RAINTREE
STECK-VAUGHN
P U B L I S H E R S
The Steck-Vaughn Company

Austin, Texas

In 1994 Nelson Mandela became president of South Africa. Before this, he had worked and suffered for freedom for his country for many years. He was the son of a Thembu chief and a great-great-grandson of the King of all the Thembus. But by the time Mandela was born, white South Africans ruled the country instead of the African tribal kings.

Whites had taken most of the good land for themselves. This made the African tribes poor. Whites made all the rules. These rules were almost impossible for blacks to live with. Mandela spent almost thirty years in prison before he could make South Africa free and fair for all its people.

As a child, Nelson Mandela slept each night in
a one-room, round hut. He slept beside his parents
and three sisters, each on their own woven mat.
His mother had three traditional huts for her
family. One was for sleeping, another for cooking,
and another for storing grain. Like most other
married women in the tribe, she had a *kraal*,
or cattle pen, for her milk cows. She planted
a garden so that she could feed her family.

The main food for the tribe was *mealies*, a kind of corn. Nelson's mother ground up the fresh corn to make *mealie-pap*. This was baked on a grate over a fire pit in the cooking hut. She and Nelson's sisters also ground dry corn into cornmeal. Nelson helped herd the cattle and goats.

Sometimes Nelson and his friends would go
hunting together. If they hit a bird, they would
pluck off its feathers and cook it right on the spot,
making a hot little snack for themselves. It was a
happy life, but when Nelson was ten years old,
his father died.

Nelson went to live with his cousin Chief Jongintaba and his family. The chief promised to take good care of Nelson and send him to school. But Nelson's most important lessons did not come from school. In those days, young people sat quietly and listened to their elders. Chiefs from all around the Thembu kingdom came to visit Chief Jongintaba.

The oldest of these chiefs was Zwelibhangile Joyi. He told Chief Jongintaba about how the Thembu kings had fought with one another and with the British. Nelson listened. He learned why the Thembus no longer owned their own land. In fact, they were poorer than they had ever been. Nelson knew he would have to work hard if he wanted to make life better for his people.

In 1941, Nelson went to Johannesburg, the biggest city in South Africa. He got a job as a gold mine policeman and learned what life was like outside the tribe. The whites-only Nationalist government said the races had to be separate. They called this idea apartheid (uh-PAR-tate). Most whites lived in big, beautiful houses in whites-only towns and cities. They often had black servants.

Black people had to get special permits to live or work in towns and cities. Most of them lived in blacks-only townships. These were usually in dry places where it was hard to grow food. There was no running water, no electricity or telephones. Blacks were not allowed to own land or vote. This was the law even though there were six or seven black people in the country for every white person.

Outside of the cities, there were few jobs. Black people with work permits had to be out of the cities by sunset every day. They had to crowd onto trains and buses. Then they traveled many hours to their townships. The next day they had to get up before dawn to travel back to work. Blacks were poorly paid and many went hungry.

Later Nelson Mandela went to the University of the Witwatersrand. He found people of all races studying together there. They talked about new ways to run South Africa. Most white people thought whites should run the country. But many students and others wanted equal rights for South African people of all languages, races, and tribes.

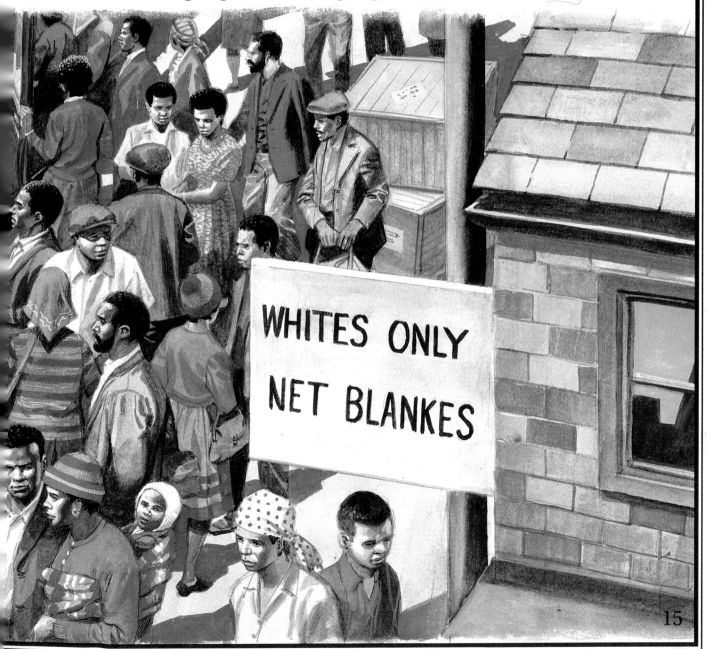

Nelson Mandela decided to spend his life getting fair government for everyone in South Africa. In 1944, at age twenty-six, he joined the African National Congress, or ANC. He also married his first wife, Evelyn.

By 1947, he had been elected secretary of the ANC Youth League. In 1951, the Youth League helped to lead a work strike. Lots of African and Indian people, who were also treated unfairly by whites, refused to work.

Later, in 1951, Mandela became president of the Youth League. He was arrested with about twenty other people for speaking out against, or protesting about, unfair laws. But they had not done anything wrong, so the South African police had to let them go.

Then people began to fight about the laws. Whites and Africans were killed. So the government stopped Mandela from even talking about the laws. It looked as if Mandela and the ANC had lost their fight.

Even so, Mandela did not give up. He carried on working for equal rights and was arrested again. In 1956, he was tried for treason, along with 155 others. Treason means working against the government. Mandela and twenty-nine others faced the death penalty, but the judge found them innocent. All 156 were set free.

His marriage to Evelyn broke up. In 1958, he married Winnie Madikizela. She joined him in the fight for freedom and justice in South Africa.

Then, in 1960, a terrible thing happened. A crowd of people were peacefully protesting about unfair laws in the town of Sharpeville. The police started to shoot at them. Sixty-nine people were killed. Another 180 men, women, and children were injured.

The government banned the ANC. This meant it was against the law to belong to it. Nelson Mandela was among those sent to prison. The government was punishing him for supporting the protesters in Sharpeville. When he was freed, Mandela and others set up a new group. Now they fought apartheid by blowing up government buildings. They made sure no one got killed. But they were not peaceful protesters anymore.

Mandela hid from police, sometimes pretending to be a chauffeur. But he was arrested in 1962. He was sentenced to five years hard labor in Pretoria Prison. While he was still in prison, he was taken to court again. This time he was sentenced to life in prison.

On June 13, 1964, he was sent to Robben Island.
The guards made him build his own prison cell.
At first, Mandela and the other political prisoners
were forced to stay in their cells day and night.
Finally, they were allowed out, but they had to
work sewing mailbags. If they talked to one another,
they lost their meals for one day.

All the time Nelson Mandela was in jail, black South Africans kept on protesting against apartheid. It took great courage. Many were killed or imprisoned. The rest of the world did not approve of keeping Mandela in prison, either. People from many countries worked to free him. They too wanted to free South Africa from apartheid. So they started to put pressure on South Africa to change.

South Africa was not allowed to join in sporting events like the Olympic Games. In 1986, the U.S. Congress passed a law to stop South African airlines from landing in the United States. The law also stopped the United States from buying many important South African products.

On Mandela's 70th birthday a huge concert was shown on television all over the world. The South African government could no longer ignore what other people thought of them.

In October 1989, F. W. de Klerk was elected president of South Africa. He began working to make South Africa a fairer place for all its people. Then, in a live worldwide television broadcast, he said that Mandela would be set free.

On Sunday, February 11, 1990, Nelson Mandela walked out of prison. Now seventy-one years old, he had been in jail for 10,000 days.

He was met outside the gates by his wife, Winnie.
She had stood by him during all that time. People
all over the world were happy that he was free at
last. Freedom for Mandela meant the government
was willing to give up the unfair laws of apartheid.
People danced in the streets with joy.

F. W. de Klerk worked with Mandela and the ANC. Together, they set up the first free elections for a new government. In 1994, Nelson Mandela ran for president. Millions of black people stood in long lines for hours in the sun. They were going to vote for the first time in their lives. Mandela won the election, and F. W. de Klerk became a deputy president.

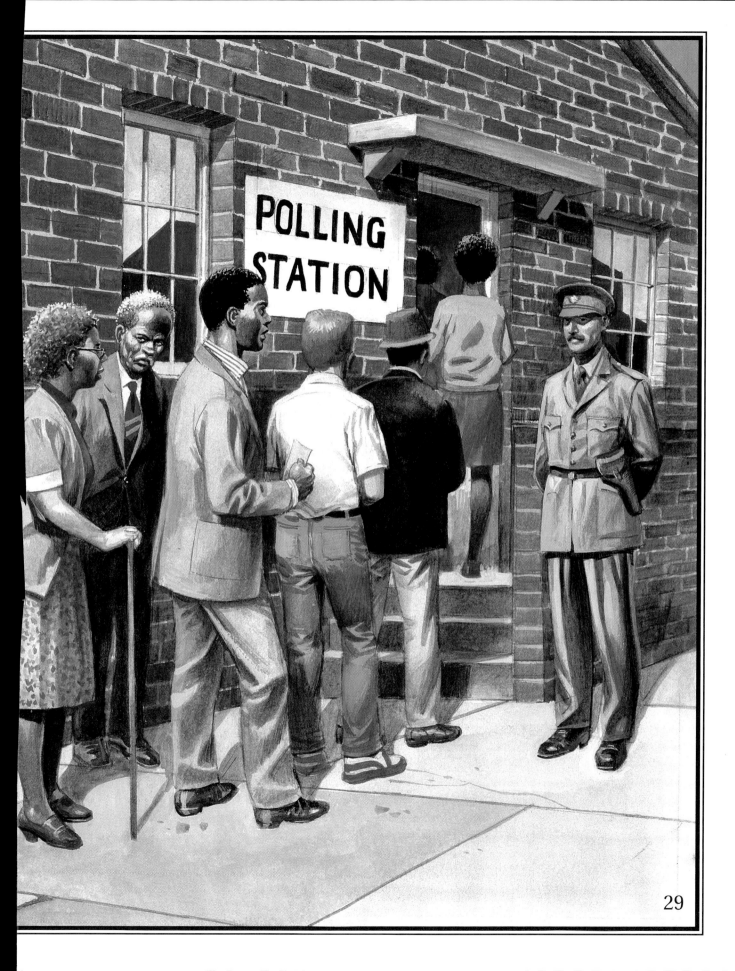

Now, President Mandela travels and meets foreign leaders, like President Clinton. He works peacefully with all his people, white and black. He wants to make a good, fair life for all South Africans. Now everyone can vote. Everyone is allowed to own property and move freely from place to place. People of all colors can begin to have jobs with equal pay for equal work. Mandela — and South Africa — are finally free.

Key Dates

1918 Born in the Transkei, a region in southeastern South Africa.

1942 Earns law degree from University of South Africa.

1944 Joins African National Congress (ANC).

1956 Treason trial for Mandela and 155 others on trial with him.

1958 Marries Nomzamo Winifred Madikizela.

1960 Peaceful protesters are shot down in Sharpeville on March 21.
The ANC is banned. Mandela and others are sent to prison.

1961 Helps start a new group that bombs government buildings.

1962 Is arrested and sentenced to five years in prison.

1964 Sentenced with eight others to life in prison.

1990 Finally freed from prison after twenty-seven years.

1991 Elected ANC president.

1994 Elected president of South Africa.